Ethereum
Learn Fast!
What you need to know to make money in an hour

While every precaution has been taken in the preparation of this book, the publisher assumes no responsibility for errors or omissions, or for damages resulting from the use of the information contained herein.

ETHEREUM - LEARN FAST - WHAT YOU NEED TO KNOW TO MAKE MONEY IN AN HOUR

First edition. April 3, 2018.

Copyright © 2018 Daniel Reed.

Written by Daniel Reed.

Copyright 2017 by Daniel Reed - All rights reserved.

This document is geared towards providing exact and reliable information in regards to the topic and issue covered. The publication is sold with the idea that the publisher is not required to render accounting, officially permitted, or otherwise, qualified services. If advice is necessary, legal or professional, a practiced individual in the profession should be ordered.

From a Declaration of Principles which was accepted and approved equally by a Committee of the American Bar Association and a Committee of Publishers and Associations.

In no way is it legal to reproduce, duplicate, or transmit any part of this document in either electronic means or in printed format. Recording of this publication is strictly prohibited and any storage of this document is not allowed unless with written permission from the publisher. All rights reserved.

The information provided herein is stated to be truthful and consistent, in that any liability, in terms of inattention or otherwise, by any usage or abuse of any policies, processes, or directions contained within is the solitary and utter responsibility of the recipient reader. Under no circumstances will any legal responsibility or blame be held against the publisher for any reparation, damages, or monetary loss due to the information herein, either directly or indirectly.

Respective authors own all copyrights not held by the publisher.

The information herein is offered for informational purposes solely, and is universal as so. The presentation of the information is without contract or any type of guarantee assurance.

The trademarks that are used are without any consent, and the publication of the trademark is without permission or backing by the trademark owner. All trademarks and brands within this book are for clarifying purposes only and are the owned by the owners themselves, not affiliated with this document.

Introduction

Ethereum is a platform that runs on a network of nodes (computers), which make certain that information and special computer applications known as smart contracts are duplicated and processed – even with the absence of a centralized server. If you haven't understood a thing of what you have just read, don't worry. You will later learn more about Ethereum and how you can make money out of it.

Ethereum is a project that was supported through a crowdfunding effort in 2014, and it is now being developed by the Ethereum Foundation - a non-profit organization based in Switzerland.

In this book, you will learn the skills you need to make sure that investing in Ethereum through holding or trading Ether tokens will be worthwhile. Specifically, you will get to know:

- How Ethereum works and how it is different compared to the blockchain technology used in Bitcoin

- The process of Ethereum mining and how you can consider it as another option to make money in cryptocurrency

- How investors are taking hold of Ether tokens to make substantial revenue in the possible upsurge of the token's value

- Other digital currencies that show potential value aside from Bitcoin and Ether

- The future prospects of Ethereum and the current hurdles that should be resolved by the platform

For anyone who has no basic knowledge of Ethereum or even cryptocurrencies and the blockchain technology, this book can help.

I hope you enjoy it!

Chapter 1 – What is Ethereum?

It will be easier to understand the nature of Ethereum if you have background knowledge on how the Internet works.

At present, our personal profile, financial information, and passwords are mostly stored in servers and data storage controlled by big players like Google, Facebook, and Amazon. Even the articles and blogs you are reading online are stored on a cloud owned by an organization that requires fees for keeping all the data.

This arrangement has numerous advantages as these organizations employ teams of data professionals to assist in keeping and securing information and help in eliminating the costs that usually come with hosting and uptime.

But there are also loopholes with these advantages. Cyber criminals, even government agencies, can have access to your data without your permission, by hacking or controlling a third-party service. Your personal information could be leaked or even modified.

The founder of Apache Web Server, Brian Behlendorf has gone so far as calling this centralized setup the "original sin" of the Internet. Advocates like him insist that the Internet should be decentralized. They highlight the risks of having a centralized design of the World Wide Web. Well, a movement has emerged around utilizing new tools such as the blockchain technology, to help attain this objective.

One of the recent technologies that take part in this splintered movement is Ethereum. Unlike Bitcoin, which aims to replace online banking, the main objective of Ethereum is to use blockchain to disrupt online third-party services.

The Global Computer

Ethereum's goal is to be a "global computer" that would not stick to the centralized user-server setup. There are also people who argue that Ethereum will democratize the current system.

With Ethereum, nodes will replace the conventional clouds and servers. These communication points are controlled by groups of volunteers located around the world.

The objective is that Ethereum would perform the same functionality to users anywhere across the globe, allowing people to compete in providing services on top of this infrastructure.

Browsing through an application store, for instance, you will find different types of applications that can be used in every aspect of life. These applications depend on a third-party service to keep your financial information, transaction data, and other personal information in their respective clouds or servers.

If everything works according to the vision, Ethereum will allow the owner of these applications to take control of the data as well as have creative rights. The point is that third parties can no longer have access to your data, and that one entity can no longer curate or censor your applications. Again, only the owner can input changes, not any entity.

In the proposed theory, it integrates the control that users had over their data in the past with accessible insights that we're used to in the digital era. Every time you input or delete notes, every communication point on the web makes the change.

Somehow the concept has been mixed with skepticism.

Even though the applications don't seem impossible, it's uncertain which apps will actually be helpful, secure, or can be quantified – and if they will be as efficient to use as the applications we have today.

With blockchain technology, Ethereum became an open source tool that gives developers authority to create over a decentralized app. With its highest hash rate value, which is 3 TeraHash, it has a huge infrastructure. Vitalik Buterin with the help of his co-developers, Charles Hoskinson, Mihai Alisie, and Anthony Di Lorio, created Ethereum for high-grade graphics processing units.

Because Ethereum is working on blockchain networks, it also comes with the conveniences of decentralized networks such as:

- Inability of other entities to input changes on data.

- Prevention of fraudulent activities caused by cyber criminals or hackers.

- Zero percent chance of applications to be turned off or crash.

The distribution of Ethereum was made possible through a public blockchain network, which is in the form of Initial Coin Offering (ICO). In ICO, more or less 35,000 Bitcoins were traded for about 60 million. This allowed an estimated amount of $ 14 million to be raised, which comprised 14% of stocks.

Moreover, the distribution of Ethereum continues to work through an ICO, in which it works at the same time with the distribution of Ether. ETH or Ether is known as the Ethereum platform's cryptocurrency token.

In Ethereum, a blockchain introduces blocks of various scalability. At the same time, there are different kinds of user accounts that raise with 22 byte addresses. There are two kinds of accounts – the external account which is the account with private keys, and the other one is the contract account which is the account with contract codes.

The authority that controls them is one of the major distinctions between the external and contract accounts.

Contract accounts are controlled by internal codes. While they can utilize contract accounts, people need external accounts to enable contract accounts. Moreover, contract accounts are permitted to execute transactions if ordered by external accounts.

Therefore, unless triggered by external accounts, these contract accounts cannot execute their usual operations such as Random Number Generation and API calls. On the other side, the control for external accounts is handed to human users since these users can control private keys, which consequently return control to external accounts.

Smart Contracts

Smart Contracts (or the use of scripting functionality) is one of the most significant features of Ethereum platform. This allows users to produce tokens that are suitable with wallets and exchanges under a standard coin API (application programming interface).

Moreover, this shows that it can speed up the exchange of money, stocks, or property. And thereby, with the use of smart contracts, we can count on a self-operating program that facilitates orders immediately once conditions are approved. Since their works are executed through a blockchain network, they operate according to how it was programmed. They execute without the possibility of being interfered by other entities, and without the chance of censorship or downtime.

Here's an overview of a smart contract's operations:

- Initially, a code from an option contract is given into the blockchain network. Although the contract serves as the public ledger, this code is given with the security from the concealment of both parties.

- A smart contract is completed once a period expires and strike prices has been reached.

- Finally, since a smart contract was executed, regulators will start monitoring the activities of the market by utilizing the blockchain network. Nevertheless, all throughout the monitoring, regulators are required to secure the privacy of both parties.

Chapter 2 - How Ethereum Works

In terms of structure, the Ethereum blockchain is quite similar to that of Bitcoin. Both have the capacity to record the whole transaction history, and each node in the network can keep a copy of the transactions.

The main difference with the Ethereum network is that the nodes are stored in the most recent state of every smart contract on top of all Ether transactions. The platform has to monitor the status of the current data for all the applications, which includes the balance of the user, the smart contract codes, and the storage location.

When it comes to Bitcoin, the platform is using unspent transaction outputs to monitor who has how much digital currency. Even though it may seem complicated, the concept is actually quite easy to understand. Each time there is a Bitcoin transaction, the network will break the total amount as if it is fiat money issuing back Bitcoins in a manner that will make the information behave similarly to actual change.

In making future transactions, the Bitcoin platform should add up all your changes that are categorized as either unspent or spent. On the other hand, the Ethereum network uses accounts.

Similar to bank accounts, Ether tokens will appear in a digital wallet, and could be transferred into another account. The funds can be easily accessed, although the concept of continued relationship is non-existent.

The Ethereum Virtual Machine

In the Ethereum platform, each time an application is used, the network of thousands of computers will take charge of the processing. The contracts that are written in a specified smart contract programming language are compiled into the bytecode, which features the Ethereum Virtual Machine (EVM) that has the ability to execute and read.

All Ethereum nodes execute the contract using EVMs. Take note that each node in the network holds a duplicate of the transaction and smart contract record of the platform aside from monitoring the present state. Each time a user performs an action, the network nodes will agree that change has occurred.

The objective here is for the network of nodes and miners to take charge of the transfer instead of relying on third-party accounts such as banks or PayPal.

Bitcoin miners will confirm the transfer of ownership of Bitcoin from one party to another, and the EVM will execute the contract with any rules that the developer will program in the onset.

Actual calculation on the EVM can be achieved via a machine readable language. However, developers could write smart contracts in high-level languages (such as Serpent and Solidify) that are easier for people to understand.

Smart Contracts

As with most concepts in the blockchain sector, most people are also confused over smart contracts, which is an emerging technology made possible through public blockchains. It can be difficult to understand mainly because the term doesn't clearly describe the core interaction.

Even though a basic contract will define the parameters of the relationship (typically legally binding), a smart contract will enforce a relationship with cryptographic code. Smart contracts are designed with special programs that specifically execute as defined.

First developed in 1993, the concept was originally explored by Nick Szabo – a cryptographer and computer scientist. He viewed smart contracts as some sort of digital vending machine. He described how users can input value or data and the machine will deliver a specified item.

Ethereum users could send one Ether token to anyone in the network anytime through a smart contract. In this example, the user will create an agreement, defining the specifics of the data to the contract so that it can execute specific commands.

Basically, Ethereum serves as a platform that is specifically designed for establishing smart contracts.

However, these new tools are not designed to be used as standalone as they can also compose the essential elements of decentralized applications (dApps) and even entire decentralized autonomous organizations (DAOs).

It is interesting to note that the Bitcoin network was the first platform to support basic smart contracts in the sense that the network could transmit value from one party to another. The node network could only validate transactions if specific conditions are met. However, Bitcoin is quite limited in the currency use case.

In contrast, Ethereum replaces the more restrictive design of Bitcoin and instead uses a programming language, which enables anyone with the right skillset to write their own applications. The network enables developers to program their own smart contracts or also known as autonomous agents. The programming language is regarded as a Turing complete, which means it can support a wider range of instructions and calculations.

Smart contracts can also serve as accounts for multi-signature so that the funds will only be spent if consensus has been reached. It can also take care of agreements between users and store details relevant to the app like membership records or domain registration.

Furthermore, smart contracts are likely to require assistance from other individual smart contracts. If someone will place a standard bet to project the temperature during a summer day, it could trigger a series of contracts under the hood. A contract will use external data to figure out the weather, and another contract will settle the bet according to the information it has received from the first contract once the conditions are met.

Running every contract will require transaction costs in form of Ether tokens that is largely based on the level of computational capacity required. The platform will execute the smart contracts using bytecode or a sequence of 1s and 0s, which could be read by the platform.

Chapter 3 – The Technology behind Ethereum

The Ethereum network allows developers to build and use decentralized applications (dApps) that serve specific purposes to its users. For example, Bitcoin is a form of dApp that provides users with a peer-to-peer electronic cash system that allows online Bitcoin payments. DApps are composed of code that are running on a blockchain network and not controlled by any central entity or individual.

With Ethereum, any centralized services could be decentralized. Consider all intermediary services, which exist across different industries – from conventional services (such as loans offered by financial institutions) to intermediary services (like regulatory compliance, voting systems, and title registries).

The Ethereum network can also be used in building decentralized autonomous organizations (DAOs), which are completely independent and have no centralized authority. These are operated by programming code, on a collection of smart contracts integrated in the Ethereum blockchain. The code is programmed to alter the structure and rules of a conventional organization to get rid of the need for centralized regulation. A DAO is owned by everyone who buy tokens, but tokens are equal to ownership and equity shares. The tokens serve as a symbol of contribution that grants people with voting rights.

Ethereum Decentralized Platform - The Pros

Since dApps are running using blockchain technology, they can also take advantage of its beneficial properties. This includes:

- Zero downtime – applications never go down and could never be switched off.

- Security – With no centralized point of failure and improved security through cryptography, decentralized applications are well protected against fraudulent activities and hack attempts.

- Tamper and corruption proof – Applications are based on a network that is built around the concept of consensus, making censorship impossible.

- Immutability – no third party can alter the data in the application

Ethereum Decentralized Platform - The Cons

Even though Ethereum offers numerous advantages, it's not 100% foolproof. Remember, the code for smart contracts is written by humans, so they are only as good as the programmers. Oversights or code bugs could lead to unintended adverse effects. If a bug in the code is taken advantage, there is no surefire way of preventing the attack other than getting a network consensus and then reprogramming the root code. This is against the core concept of blockchain, given that it's designed to be immutable. In addition, any action that is taken by a centralized party could raise serious questions about the decentralized nature of an application.

Developing a Decentralized Application in the Ethereum Network

There are several ways that you could plug into the Ethereum platform. Among the easiest ways is using the native Mist browser that provides a basic interface and online wallet for storing and trading Ether and to create, manage, and store smart contracts. Similar to browsers that provide access and help people to browse the internet, Mist offers a portal into the world of dApps.

Another extension is MetaMask, which converts Google Chrome into the Ethereum platform. MetaMask enables anyone to easily develop and run dApps from their browser. While it is originally designed as a Chrome plugin, MetaMask will gradually be available for Firefox and a range of other web browsers.

Although these are still on beta version, MetaMask, Mist, and other browsers are set to make blockchain applications more accessible in the coming years. Even users without technical background could easily build blockchain applications, which is a significant development for blockchain technology and could raise dApps into mainstream use.

Current Applications Being Developed in the Ethereum Network

People can use the Ethereum network to develop applications across a wide range of industries and services. However, developers are exploring a new field, so it can be difficult to figure out the applications that will succeed or fail. Below are some interesting applications that are presently in the Ethereum network:

- Augur – This open-source application is designed to predict events and receive rewards for correct forecasts. Predictions on future real world events such as who will become the next US President, are implemented through virtual shares. When a user purchases shares in a winning prediction, they can receive monetary rewards.

- Provenance – This application harnesses the power of the Ethereum network to improve the transparency of opaque supply chains. By keeping the origins and record of products, the project can build an accessible and open framework of information so consumers could make informed decisions when they purchase products.

- BlockApps – Provides an easy platform for businesses to build, manage, and use blockchain applications. From integration with legacy systems to full production and proof of concept, this app offers all the tools needed to develop private, semi-private, and public industry-specific blockchain apps.

- Uport – This application provides users with a convenient and secure way to take charge of personal information online. Users can control who can access and use their personal information instead of depending on government agencies or entrusting their personal data to third parties.

- Weifund – This open application provides an easy platform for crowdfunding campaigns that harness the power of smart contracts. It allows contributions to be converted into contractual-based digital assets, which could be used or traded inside the Ethereum platform.

The 2016 DAO Attack

At this point, you should already know the fact that the Ethereum network can be used to build DAOs. Well, in 2016, a DAO has been compromised due to a hacking attack. A startup company developed a DAO to provide a humanless venture capital service, which aims to help investors make decisions through the aid of smart contracts. The DAO was financed via an ICO and ended up raising about $150 Million from investors around the world.

Upon raising funds, The DAO software was hacked by cyber criminals who took Ether worth around $50 Million during that time. Although the negligence was not on the side of the Ethereum platform but because of the technical flaw in the system of DAO software, the executives of Ethereum were obliged to address the mess created by the attack.

After all the discussions, the Ethereum community came to an agreement to recover $50 million dollars' worth of Ether by making a change in the code – a process also known as a hard fork. The change in code moved the robbed funds to a fresh smart contract created to allow the original owners to draw back their tokens. However, the ramification of this decision is still controversial and debatable.

Ethereum is based on the blockchain network wherein every action recorded is irrevocable and permanent. By changing a code and writing the rules by which blockchains operate, Ethereum made a risky precedent that contradicts the very purpose of blockchain. If blockchain is modified every time a huge amount of money is involved or a number of users get affected, the major value proposition of blockchain (secure, anonymous, tamper-proof, and unchangeable) will be lost

While a fork was put forth, the Ethereum community and its executives were trapped in a perilous situation. If they failed to recover the robbed fund of the investors, trust in Ethereum could be lost. On the other side, retrieving the fund of the investors set actions that go against the main essence of decentralization and require a risky precedent.

At end of the day, the Ethereum Community came to a consensus to execute the hard fork and recover the stolen funds of DAO investors. But not all agreed with their decision. This lead to a division, creating the two parallel blockchains that now exist.

Ethereum Classic (ETC) is available for those who went against the hard fork. Ethereum (ETH) is available for most members of the network who voted yes to change a minor part of the blockchain and issue a refund to the rightful owners.

Ethereum Classic and Ethereum both have similar features and are essentially the same in every way, up to a certain part where the blockchain was rewritten or changed. This only shows that all that occurred on Ethereum up until the change in code is still valid on the Ethereum Classic blockchain. From the part where the hard fork was performed onwards, the two blockchains work separately.

Despite the controversies from the DAO software hack, Ethereum is still looking forward to big opportunities. By giving a user-friendly platform that allows users to equip the functions of blockchain technology, it is now helping in quickening the decentralization of the world economy. Apps that went through decentralization have the possibility to completely disrupt entire industries such as insurance, academia, real estate, health care, finance, and many more.

Chapter 4 - What is Ethereum Mining?

Currently, miners play a vital role in making Ethereum work effectively. Although, this role is not really obvious.

Many people assume that the essence of mining is to provide Ethereum tokens in a manner that does not stand in need of a central issuer. It's actually correct. At a rate of 5 tokens for every block mined, Ethers are obtained through the process of mining. However mining also has other important roles aside from generating the cryptocurrency.

Oftentimes, banks are responsible of storing accurate records of transactions. Banks make sure that money is not produced out of nowhere, and the people don't pay out their money more than once.

Although blockchains introduced a totally new form of storing records, one where the whole web (instead of an intermediary) confirms transactions and records them to the public ledger. While a 'trustless' financial system is the objective, somebody still requires to secure the financial data to preserve the accuracy of records.

One innovation that makes decentralized registration possible is mining.

Miners agree about the transaction record while avoiding fraud or cheats – an issue that had not been addressed in decentralized currencies before proof-of-work blockchains.

Ethereum, though, is finding other means of coming to an agreement about the genuineness of transactions – and mining is what's presently controlling the platform.

How Ethereum Mining Works

Ethereum and Bitcoin have almost identical mining processes.

In every block of transaction, miners utilize computers to frequently and immediately guess answers to a puzzle until someone wins.

The miners will operate the group's unique header metadata (like software version and timestamp) with a mixed-up function, only modifying the node value which affects the outcome of the hash value.

The miner will gain Ether upon finding a hash compatible with the current target. They will announce the block all over the network for every node to confirm and record to their own copy of the ledger. For example, if miner B discovers the hash, miner A will pause from processing on the current block and repeat the course for the next block.

It's hard for miners to cheat the process. It is impossible to fake this game and get the right puzzle answer. That is the reason why the puzzle-solving method is referred as 'proof-of-work'. On the other hand, it's so easy for other miners to confirm that the hash value is right.

Ideally, a miner recovers a block within 12 to 15 seconds. The algorithm will immediately change the problem's level of difficulty if this timeframe isn't being maintained. The miners randomly obtain Ether tokens and their gains rely on luck and the volume of computing power they allotted to it.

Ethash is a specialized proof-of-work algorithm that Ethereum is currently using. This algorithm demands massive memory, making it more difficult to mine utilizing costly Application-Specific Integrated Circuits (ASICs), which are designed especially for mining and are currently the sole profitable means of mining bitcoin.

In essence, it might have succeeded in that objective, since there is no available ASICs to mine Ethereum. Moreover, because Ethereum aims to shift from proof-of-work to proof-of-stake (which you will later learn), using an ASIC may not be an ideal option because it may not prove useful for long.

Top Benefits of Mining Ether

While it's proven that mining Ethereum is cost-effective, it might not be a smart option for those who simply want to obtain the currency. It's better for them to focus on buying Ethereum. Still, is it profitable to mine Ethereum? The answer is yes. Certainly, you can obtain Ethereum with low-power Graphics Processing Units (GPUs). Despite this, the price of Ethereum is still increasing.

It is projected that with a GPU (specifically Radeon R9-295-X2), you can possibly earn over $1,000 for every card each year, which shows that you can still break even before the year ends and start earning passively.

Because Ethereum's value is gradually increasing, your income margin will definitely increase even more. In many ways, the Ethereum network is similar to the Bitcoin network. However, it has two primary distinctions that are crucial for its progress: smart contracts and the shift to proof-of-stake.

Smart Contracts

Not similar to Bitcoin, the programming language used for writing Ethereum makes it more possible for developers to make 'programmable money' or smart contracts. The cryptocurrency world sees this as a revolutionary innovation and has paved the way for numerous opportunities to further develop the field.

Transition to Proof-of-Stake

The transition of Ethereum from proof-of-work (POW) to proof-of-stake (POS) is its second main distinction from Bitcoin. Understanding POW is crucial in order for you to understand POS.

The technology of blockchain was developed in 2009, the same year that Bitcoin was introduced. In this sense, blockchain can be considered as a kind of database and in the cryptocurrency world, the database of transaction is the blockchain. If a user tries to start a flawed transaction, the code of blockchain will detect that it is not valid and so will not permit its processing.

Basically, in mining a cryptocurrency like Ethereum, Litecoin, or Bitcoin, a user sets up a computer (or networks of computers) to answer the algorithm of the cryptocurrency.

The computers processing the transactions are doing extremely hard operations. Basically, the computer has to frequently check the code until it discovers the answer in order to confirm an acceptable transaction on a blockchain.

There are several flaws in the proof-of-work scheme. This includes:

- A high amount of initial investment in purchasing costly computers
- This system consumes huge amounts of power for mining
- Electricity expenses are costly and could easily eat up your income

Electricity expense is a crucial factor you need to consider in Ethereum mining. The needed electricity cost to support all Ethereum miners can be higher compared to the total power cost of a small country. In the long run, this flaw will bring a huge problem. In the next few years, there will be an increase in the power needed to mine.

Proof of Stake (POS)

By shifting into POS, you can already monitor the coins that you have using your wallet or your computer. For instance, if the network has 500 tokens and you stake 50 of your total coins, you will gain 10 percent of the deposits being staked. Therefore you will gain 10 percent of the total tokens from the platform.

Instead of mining coins, you're staking it – and in doing so, you are actually locking your coins.

If you forge any transactions or if you don't confirm it, you will lose the tokens you locked in the networks.

The Benefits of POS

Electricity is not needed in POS, as the GPUs don't need to perform any cryptographic hashes. It has eliminated the need to spend a lot of money on electricity or hardware. If your goal is to gain rewards, you need to secure your coins. With POW, you are actually using electricity to convert into coins. With POS, you are making coins out of coins.

Is Ethereum Mining Profitable?

Notwithstanding the use or relevance of the smart contracts, a lot of cryptocurrency advocates and stakeholders like the concept. This contributes to the increasing price of Ethereum.

There are clear long-term advantages when it comes to a POS system implemented in the Ethereum network. It will help in saving electricity. It can also eliminate or reduce the hardware expenses.

Nevertheless, mining will still become a lucrative venture in the next few years. The conversion to POS isn't common (yet it is leading its way to mainstream adoption), and we are still relying on Ethereum mining to confirm the transaction in the blockchains. POS and smart contracts will help boost and increase Ethereum's value, making it a highly profitable cryptocurrency to mine.

Chapter 5 - How to Mine Ethereum

You can use any PC to mine Ethereum, but never use light devices with underpowered GPUs (such as laptops). Ethereum mining using the CPU is not practical. It takes a longer period to complete the process, but the revenue is lower compared to expenses.

When it comes to mining, GPUs are better than CPUs – and GPUs are at least 200 times faster than a typical CPU. Do note though, that nVidia cards are slower compared to AMD cards. If you're familiar with these cards' mainstream applications, you're probably wondering why AMD's offerings are considered superior. After all, nVidia is deemed better in almost every application there is. This is due to the fact that the main mining program for Ether is implemented in OpenCL – a software framework fully supported by AMD's GPUs. While nVidia GPUs can still work with the open-source framework, they're actually optimized for CUDA (the company's own version of OpenCL).

Indeed it takes a high volume of electricity in order to mine Ether. If mining is executed efficiently, an increase in profits can be gained by selling Ether tokens.

To be sure of your plan's profitability, you might need to use specialized mining calculators. There are also Ethereum Mining mini-computers for determining profits.

The Ethereum Mining Process

Below is a simple process to set-up your Ethereum mining node and begin mining your first Ether token.

Step 1 - Download Geth

The first thing that you need to do is establish your communication channel. You need to download a software called Geth. This will create a secure connection to the Ethereum network across the world while it coordinates your hardware. It'll provide updates on the processes being done, particularly those that need response from your end.

Geth is often downloaded as a Zip file, which you'll have to extract somewhere. It is ideal to use your C drive for this step. Use the Windows search option to look for CMD. If you are not certain, then you can browse around the search listing.

Step 2 - Locate Geth

The placeholder for the username is often similar to the system name (e.g. C:\Users\Username>). In locating Geth, you need to type in *cd/* in cmd. This is a command to shift directory. *C:\>* should be on highlight, which shows that you are in drive C.

Step 3 - Create an Account

At this point, you should start creating your user account. To do this, start by making a call: type in *geth account new* then press Enter. *C:\>geth account new* should be displayed now in the command prompt. This step also involves setting up your password. You need to be cautious in setting your password, and be sure that you use a strong combination of alphanumeric keys. After keying in the password, press Enter and you now have a new account.

Step 4 - Download Ethereum Blockchain

Linking the Geth to the Ethereum network is needed before it becomes functional. Type in *geth — RPC* on the command terminal before pressing the Enter key. This activity begins with downloading the Ethereum blockchain and linking with the world's blockchain. This action is time consuming and relies on the size of the blockchain. It also relies on your web connection speed. Be sure to wait until it's done before proceeding.

Step 5 - Install Ethminer

Now, you need to install a program that will allow the GPU to operate the blockchain algorithm needed in the Ethereum network. The ideal option for this difficult task is Ethminer. Create a fresh terminal for command then access the terminal icon (active) that is located on the taskbar before accessing the terminal window in the menu.

In the newly opened terminal window, put *cd prog* then press tab. *C:\>cd prog* must appear in the window, press tab to show *C:/> cd "Program Files"* then press Enter to display *C:\Program Files>*.

Type *cd cpp* and press Enter in order to proceed to the Ethereum mining folder. The terminal window will show *C:\Program Files\cpp-ethereum>* right after you press tab again.

Step 6 - Start Mining

Key in *Ethminer –G* on your terminal window then press the Enter key in order to start mining with your GPU. This will start Ethereum mining after the Directed Acyclic Graph (DAG) gets created. It's a huge file mainly kept in your

GPU's RAM so it can be compatible with ASIC. Nonetheless, you have to ensure that your HDD has sufficient space before doing this step.

If necessary, mining Ether using a CPU is also possible. Just type *ETHMINER* then push the Enter key to initiate the mining process. The creation of DAG is necessary in this phase, after which the connection with Ethminer will be taken over by Geth.

Chapter 6 - Investing in Ethereum

Part of the massive popularity of cryptocurrencies in 2017 is Ethereum. It is a decentralized system, which disrupts the need for third-parties or banks in sending payments across the internet.

The total market value of cryptocurrencies increased to more than $200 billion. These alternative currencies even entered the mainstream with the introduction of the first Bitcoin Futures on the Chicago Board Options Exchange. So, here are some reasons why you should invest in Ethereum.

1. It is growing in popularity

In a span of two years, Ethereum managed to establish itself as one of the fastest growing digital currencies in the market, second only to the largest digital currency in the world. The idea of Ethereum was first proposed by a 19 year old, Vitalik Buterin, in 2013. Presently, millions of people have already obtained this currency, though many say that the idea of having third-party apps that can run on their network is its main attraction.

2. Ethereum's value is rising

Ether, the valuation of Ethereum's currency, has gradually increased these past months as people have started setting up their own cryptocurrency wallets. It has been used for public trades since 2016 and the release of Ether is only limited to eighteen million every twelve months. These days, it isn't surprising at all to see a single Ether being valued at more than 700 USD.

3. Ether could be the future of currency

Ethereum and other digital currencies have the capacity to innovate and transform the financial system, in the same way Airbnb and Uber have done in their own field. Confidence in conventional markets is low given the emergence of a financial crisis ten years ago, and people are now becoming more confident with what the online world has to offer.

4. You can trade on exchanges

It's a good thing to have options as there are numerous cryptocurrency exchanges that allow Ethereum on their platform. One of the most distinguished, Coinbase, faces competition from exchanges like the Buy Virtual Currency. This new platform offers individual account managers and effective customer service – all while accepting almost every digital currency available.

5. You can already use ETH to pay for products and services

More and more businesses are starting to accept digital currency as payment. Also, as people become more comfortable with cryptocurrencies, it's to be expected that the number of organizations that will get involved with Ether will rise over the next few years. In fact, Overstock.com, an online retailer of furniture, bedding, and DIY, which is located near Salt Lake City, notified their customers that they are already accepting cryptocurrencies as payment.

Chapter 7 - How to Make Money Buying and Selling Ethereum

We could compare the current status of Ethereum to that of Bitcoin during its introduction in 2009. A man from Norway invested $27 worth of Bitcoins in 2009 and just stored it in his wallet. The next time he checked it, BTC's value had already skyrocketed to $800,000 based on the current price.

We cannot say what could happen to Ethereum after a decade, but there is a big possibility that Ethereum will outgrow Bitcoin.

Purchasing Ether Tokens for Long-term Investment

The blockchain technology, which is the underlying technology of Ethereum, can be used for different purposes built in a system that is both decentralized and autonomous from the network. It can be a groundbreaking innovation that has the power to change the landscape in many industries.

The value of Ether will continue to hike thanks to the increasing demand for the Ethereum platform and its smart contracts. The platform experienced organic growth without any danger of massive spikes, and stability is no longer an issue. The movement in the demand and price of a specific digital currency can be seen as a metric of its potential.

The developers behind the success of Ethereum like to see the web as huge global computer that helps apps operate. This is probably the reason why more investors (including Bill Gates) are supporting the project.

Paving its way to a more stable industry: Microsoft Corporation is now offering blockchain as a service. Other big companies such as IBM have already expressed their willingness to cooperate. Meanwhile, researchers from the Massachusetts Institute of Technology (MIT) are also doing active study and even offering their own alternatives to the Ethereum blockchain.

At present, Ethereum is the second largest cryptocurrency in terms of market capitalization. It's also among the leading cryptocurrencies when it comes to volume and popularity.

How and Where to Buy Ethereum

Numerous online platforms can be used to purchase digital currencies such as Ethereum. Among them is Coinbase, which is noted as a reliable and secure platform for buying and selling Ether tokens. Coinbase can be used in over 30 countries around the world including Switzerland, San Marino, Slovakia, Slovenia, Spain, Sweden, Singapore, Canada, United States, United Kingdom, Romania, Portugal, Poland, Norway, Austria, Netherlands, Belgium, Monaco, Bulgaria, Malta, Croatia, Liechtenstein, Cyprus, Latvia, Czech republic, Italy, Denmark, Ireland, Finland, Hungary, France, and Greece.

In 2017, Coinbase has become the world's biggest Bitcoin dealer. It is now possible to invest in Ethereum and Bitcoin using your bank account or through other payment methods such as Interact Online and SEPA transfer.

In Coinbase, buyers can easily purchase or sell digital currencies of their choice. It's so user-friendly that it is possible for the users to purchase Ethereum and Bitcoin instantly with a debit card or credit card.

In case you are still in doubt if it is really reliable, Coinbase is located in California and is supported by institutional investors and venture capitalists.

Here are the steps on how to set up a Coinbase account

Step 1 - The first thing you need to do is sign up for a Coinbase account, so you can have a secure place where you can store your digital currency and exchange your fiat currency into cryptocurrencies.

Step 2 - After signing up, link a valid bank account, debit card, or credit card to the platform. You just need to complete a simple verification process so you can start using your account.

Step 3 - After buying your first digital currency, the platform will fulfill the process of purchasing and delivering your Ether tokens. The value of Ether varies over time. The price may go up or down, so Coinbase will update you of the prevailing exchange rate before you confirm the transaction.

These days, Ether's value when converted to fiat currency might be high but this could still be the ideal time to get involved in the trade – especially if you take a closer look at Ethereum's price chart.

Is It Possible to Make Money in Ethereum in Just An Hour?

Actually, yes. With the right knowledge, skills, and equipment, thousands of people have already made money from buying and selling Ether tokens. A small movement in the market can bring thousands of dollars into your pocket.

After setting up your account with Bitcoin exchanges such as Coinbase, you can start buying Ether tokens. Take note that there is no need to buy tokens in full units. You can purchase tokens even in fractions at present prices. This makes cryptocurrencies such as Ether easy targets for speculation.

Most cryptocurrency exchanges such as Coinbase don't charge for transferring the digital currency from one user to another, which is the main concept of the blockchain technology. However, if you like to send money to your bank account, the exchange will charge a minimal conversion fee, which is usually 3.99% if you are using a debit or credit card or 1.49% if you are using bank account. So try to stay away from using credit cards unless you can receive enough reward points to offset the expensive charges.

After trading some Ether tokens in Coinbase, you can choose to level up to the bigger platforms such as the Global Digital Asset Exchange (GDAX), which is the Coinbase's advanced day trading service. You can use the same credentials with Coinbase, and you can easily send the digital tokens between the platforms that can really provide convenience. GDAX offers an interactive interface with real-time pricing data, a simplified buy-sell order process, as well as trade history, charting tools, and order book features.

Most day traders who are already comfortable with GDAX have completely stopped day trading through Coinbase's primary platform. GDAX also charges cheaper transaction fees compared to Coinbase, which range between 0.1% and 0.25% for buyers and surprisingly no charge for sellers. But take note that fees vary according to the monthly trade volume.

The primary benefit of the Coinbase system is that it provides a simpler interface and the order is guaranteed to fill, in exchange for a higher fee. Sellers don't need to pay any charges on GDAX, but there is a risk that the order may not be filled and you have to work on a new set price.

Learn How to Read Charts and Look for Trends

If you are convinced that the cryptocurrency market will increase in value in the near future, then your strategy is to collect as much as coins as you can. Include the right cryptocurrencies to diversify your portfolio so you can make money over time.

One strategy to do this is to purchase tokens during a downtrend and allow the profits to roll over. It is best to enter and exit positions slowly in case the trend behaves contrary to market prediction. Stay away from trading in huge emotional or reactionary swings and avoid trading several times a week so you can minimize your fees.

Another way to determine if the Ether stock price is undervalued or overvalued is by reading the moving averages, which you can find on the stock charts. This will help in smoothing out volatility and figuring out the direction of Ether.

More often than not, short-term moving averages (usually represented in red line) can cross over long-term moving averages (usually represented in black line). This is usually succeeded with a spike in the price movement. You must also take a closer look at the spikes in the trade volume, as this could indicate great sentiments of excitement or fear in the market.

Chapter 8 - Ethereum and Other Cryptocurrencies

Ethereum is now the second biggest cryptocurrency in the world, only next to Bitcoin. Some advocates even believe that this digital currency is well positioned to soon take over BTC.

However, it's a wise investment strategy to never put all your eggs in one basket. The classic method of diversification is still applicable when it comes to your cryptocurrency holdings. As such, it's necessary to learn about other cryptocurrencies that show potential.

Bitcoin Cash (BCH)

For a short period in the last quarter of 2017, disagreement rose among the adopters of Bitcoin over the technical restrictions of Bitcoin. This has resulted to a hard fork in the blockchain, which in turn resulted to the introduction of Bitcoin Cash (BCH).

Some disappointed cryptocurrency miners decided to fork the token by using a new software, with the primary objective of scaling the cryptocurrency. Since its introduction, the new token has secured its ranking among the top digital currencies, without the need to take over Bitcoin when it comes to buzz, value, and usage. BCH has an estimated market cap of more than $28 Billion.

Monero (XMR)

Another decentralized and open-source digital currency is the Monero. This private and untraceable currency was released in the first quarter of 2014.

In just a short period, it managed to generate interest within the cryptography community. It easily convinced countless traders and enthusiasts to invest. The progress of Monero is purely community-driven and donation-based.

This digital currency has been introduced to focus on scalability and decentralization. It allows extra security by applying a special cryptographic technique called "ring signatures". In this technique, a set of cryptographic signatures is shown (including the one which is the real participant), but since every signature in the set seems valid, the real one cannot be identified.

Cardano (ADA)

Originally, Cardano is a platform used for transferring digital currency. It facilitates storage and transfer of value through its ADA token. Like Ether, the network of Cardano aims to operate decentralized applications in the blockchain. The network was developed by a co-founder of the Ethereum Network, Charles Hopkins. It is also regarded as the Ethereum of Japan since around 95% of its ICOs were raised from the country. The network is currently administered by a global group of academics and scientists who specialize in blockchain applications. Cardano's market capitalization is estimated to be around $16 Billion.

Ripple (XRP)

Ripple is a cryptocurrency launched in 2012. It now has a market capitalization of $1.26 billion. The said digital currency is a real-time global settlement network that gives immediate, certain, and affordable international payments. It enables banking organizations and similar financial institutions to manage payments across geographical borders in near real-time (if not real-time) at a very low cost.

Ripple's structure doesn't require mining using GPU or CPU, thereby it decreases dependency on computational capacity and reduces network latency. Ripple's developers insist that dispensing price is an effective method of rewarding particular behaviors and so, they're planning to distribute the tokens through deals and institutional investments.

Dash (DASH)

A more secretive version of Bitcoin was launched in the first quarter of 2014. The Dash (also known as Darkcoin) was created and developed by Evan Duffield. In 2015, Darkcoin was renamed to Dash which means Digital Cash. It can be mined using a GPU or CPU.

The change on its name did not affect any of its technological features like InstantX and Darksend, It still gives anonymity as it executes on a decentralized mastercode web that makes transactions almost untraceable. Dash is now being used by a lot people around the globe.

Zcash (ZEC)

In the last quarter of 2016, an open-source and decentralized digital currency was released. It was the Zcash. It was referred to as the https of money, while Bitcoin was considered the http. Zcash gives privacy and selective transparency in all transactions.

Hence, Zcash still claims to give extra security wherein every transaction is noted and issued on a blockchain, but information such as the recipient, sender, and the amount is not indicated. "Shielded" transactions are being offered by this digital currency, which permit the content to be encrypted utilizing new cryptographic methods. The cryptographic technique called zk-SNARK is a zero-knowledge proof construction – this was developed by the same people behind Zcash.

Stellar (XLM)

XLM is now a major digital currency thanks to its staggering 29,400% growth last year. The XLM token is a breakaway token from Ripple and was introduced in 2014 by Jed McCaleb – a co-founder of Ripple and Jouce Kim (a former lawyer) after an internal disagreement in the Ripple network. Similar to Ripple, Stellar is a transaction platform that offers easy and fast international money transfer. Its market capitalization is estimated to be around $10.5 Billion.

Litecoin (LTC)

Released in 2011, Litecoin is one of the first digital currencies that came out after the birth of Bitcoin. Litecoin is often referred to as the silver of the cryptocurrency world. The man behind the creation of Litecoin, Charlie Lee is a graduate from Massachusetts Institute of Technology (MIT) and a former engineer at Google.

The said digital currency is patterned on an open-source global payment web that's not owned by any central authority or third party. Just like some digital currencies, it also utilizes "scrypt" as proof-of-work. Even though Litecoin is similar to Bitcoin in many ways, Litecoin has a faster rate of block generation and therefore, gives immediate transaction confirmation. Many investors (aside from developers) are now embracing LTC.

Chapter 9 - The Future of Ethereum

In the past two years, digital currencies have attracted the attention of many investors, particularly after the historic rise in popularity of digital currencies such as Ether and Bitcoin. For instance, in the latter part of 2015, a single BTC was only worth around $440, while BTC was worth around $3000 in July 2017 – and has increased to around $8,000 in November 2017.

Cryptocurrency investors project that the price of Ether can go beyond $5,000 before 2018 ends. Its price was only $10 in 2017, and now it's around $800. Of course, there are those skeptical of this prediction. Take note that in order to reach $2,000, the market cap of Ethereum should be $200 billion, and some suggest that it could even reach $2,000 in just one day.

Other investment experts also believe that Ether could reach $1,000 in value in 2020. This is seen as a very conservative estimate for the cryptocurrency. Experts are considering three main factors in forecasting price:

- Ether's demand
- Ether's application
- Ether's supply (current and future)

The demand for Ether is mainly influenced by two things. First, its usage as a currency that is built on a blockchain with different uses, and second as a possible vehicle for investment that will keep on increasing its value.

For Ether's functionality, the technology behind smart contracts is what entices people most. But in light of recent events, the establishment of new applications on top of the Ethereum blockchain can also boost demand.

Ether's unique selling point (at least when compared to Bitcoin) is its capacity to use smart contracts, which as we have discussed in the early part of this book, are contracts that are instantly executed without the need for any human input the moment their terms are met.

However, the platform also allows developers to establish decentralized applications or dApps aside from the blockchain technology. It's interesting to note that the more apps are built, the more Ether tokens increase in value. Investment experts believe that in a span of five to seven years, we can expect a 20-fold increase in the number of decentralized blockchain applications.

At present, there are around 96 million Ether coins in circulation. Even though this number is likely to increase in the next two years, it will possibly experience a plateau after. This means that the programmers behind the Ethereum project need to ensure that the number of ETH tokens in circulation will stay constant.

Ethereum May Overtake Bitcoin

Again, some cryptocurrency experts believe that Ether's price could outperform Bitcoin. Hence, a dollar invested in Ether could provide a higher ROI compared to if it were put in BTC.

Although this may seem impossible to believe in the early weeks of 2018 looking at the price of Bitcoin, we are already aware that in the last weeks, BTC price fell down to $6,000. It is possible that Bitcoin is now used by investors for short-term revenue generation. It is also important to note that the assertion is based on the rise of Ethereum between 2015 and 2017, while the assertion for BTC was between 2009 and 2017.

As a matter of fact, Olaf Carlson Wee, the Chief Executive Officer (CEO) of Polychain Capital, believes that Ethereum's market capitalization can take over Bitcoin's in 2018. There are numerous indicators showing positive support for this projection.

Basically, Bitcoin has already lost around 50% of its market share to Ethereum in the past four months. It is also interesting to note that only four months ago, 90 percent of all funds invested in digital currency was poured into BTC.

But this number has dropped to around 45%, and the share of Ethereum has increased four-fold, which puts it around the 30 percent mark.

It's also helpful to know the backers of a currency to assess if Ether can really overtake Bitcoin. The focus of Bitcoin into payment processing makes it attractive with governments such as China and Japan.

However, the smart contract technology of Ethereum make it attractive among companies who have vested interest in actual applications. For instance, a new organization dubbed as the Enterprise Ethereum Alliance (EEA) has brought up the mission of fostering and facilitating Ether's growth.

EEA is composed of more than 86 companies that include Microsoft and JP Morgan. The support from these companies significantly affect the demand of the cryptocurrency and attests to its great potential.

However, Ethereum's future is not always on the positive end. In spite of the positive leaning of the market towards Ether, the digital currency is still facing major setbacks in nailing down its survival and growth.

Primarily, Ether may have several differences compared to Bitcoin, but it is still running on blockchain technology, which means it's also vulnerable to the problems that all present blockchain technologies are facing. One of the leading concerns is scalability.

In scalability, the main concern is whether the increased number of users can significantly affect the time of transaction. To put it simply, if more people are using the technology, there will be more transactions to register and place in the ledger.

This surge in the volume of transactions could mean that any transaction has to wait in a long queue before getting added into the block. As we have lightly discussed in the earlier chapters, this problem has created a fork problem, and there is no consensus yet on solving it.

Another concern with the Ethereum network is the probability of duplicating the technology. After all, any company could begin its own digital currency that's based on blockchain anytime. The main factor that grants value in any cryptocurrency is the agreement of the community in using a particular cryptocurrency.

Hence, it can be difficult to place full trust in one digital currency without the risk of another digital currency emerging and taking over the current standing of ETH and even BTC.

Of course, these concerns, when not solved, could jeopardize the future of Ether. Therefore, it makes any price projection for Ether in the next year or so quite difficult.

On the Matter of Security

As we've mentioned several times throughout the course of this book, more and more people are choosing to invest in Ether. Now with that trend, it's only to be expected that cyber criminals will be on the lookout for opportunities to earn big – taking advantage of every security vulnerability there is.

While hot wallets (online key storage solutions typically offered by cryptocurrency exchanges) may suffice for now, you'll still have to consider eventually transitioning to a cold wallet. Keep in mind that despite the convenience offered by hot wallets (being that they can be accessed anywhere as long as you're connected to the web), they're also the most vulnerable. In other words, since your wallet is on the internet, hackers from other parts of the world may end up getting your hard-earned Ether.

Cold wallets offer increased security simply by not relying on the web. They'll only be connected whenever you make a transaction. What are cold wallets exactly? They're USB devices designed specifically to function as a storage for cryptocurrency. Most of these physical wallets even come with backup solutions for complete peace of mind.

Despite being quite impressive, cold wallets (like the Ledger Nano S) are far from perfect. For one, finding one won't be easy – they're in limited supply, and the number of people interested in Ether is continuously increasing. Clearly, these devices are going to become more expensive as well.

Although some would say that you can always print a paper-based alternative (such as through MyEtherWallet), would you really want to risk losing everything if ever your cold wallet gets crumpled or smudged? It probably won't be worth it as a permanent solution, but it should be fine for temporary use.

Conclusion

Remember, investing in any opportunity could be good, or it may not. This is true not only for Ether but also in cryptocurrency in general, and of course on your perspective as the investor or day trader.

With digital currency still in its early years, the market remains quite volatile. Take note that although this book has provided you with the most relevant information available today, this is not a professional advice and doesn't guarantee results.

Still, it is important to note that there is a major upside in cryptocurrency investment. With the sector in its nascent stage, many investors are optimistic in projecting future prices – and that will make trading a nice venture.

Even if we say that Ether and other cryptocurrencies are still in a bubble, the trend can be very well be toward the digital current being an essential storage for value and medium of exchange. This is viable for those who are looking for a good long-term investment. While this could pose a high risk for day traders, it also comes with great rewards.

If you're in the US, take note that cryptocurrencies such as Ether are already legal – meaning they're already highly regulated. And when you hold it for investment, it is taxed similar to investment property. Hence, you can keep tab of your trades, and keep them as capital gains and then work with the tax office similar to any capital investment.

Meanwhile, the specific regulations are still not clear and could easily complicate things. For instance, it is not completely clear if the regulation for like-kind property is applicable for cryptocurrencies.

If they are applicable, this means that for each trade from one digital currency to another can be a taxable event for the year. If they are not applicable, then there's no need to pay the taxes on Ether holdings until you decide to cash them out. So, it will help you a lot to study the tax considerations in investing or holding Ether coins.

Regardless of what the future may hold, remember that the main focus of this book is to equip you with the knowledge you need so you can consider Ethereum as a possible (and viable) investment opportunity, whether for the long term or simply to make money in an hour.

www.ingramcontent.com/pod-product-compliance
Lightning Source LLC
Chambersburg PA
CBHW030043230526
45472CB00005B/1653